A souvenir guide

Mottisfont

Hampshire

🦌 National Trust

The Story of Mottisfont

The beautiful setting and the spring that gave Mottisfont its name have attracted and continue to attract generation after generation. Mottisfont's story unfolds through the people who have lived and loved in this place.

Picture the peace of a prosperous mediaeval country priory with orchards, gardens, dovecotes, watermills and pastures, where pilgrims came to be blessed by Augustinian canons.

Envisage the grandeur of a Tudor country house, built on land given to his Lord Chamberlain by Henry VIII, with two courtyards, imposing chimneys and great staircase turrets.

And imagine the sparkle of interwar 20th-century house parties, where 'Bright Young Things' rubbed shoulders with writers, painters and poets, where love affairs blossomed and creativity bloomed.

Water of life
For more than 800 years people have lived and worked on the Mottisfont estate, sheltered in the valley of the River Test,

Below The 12th-century Augustinian priory was converted into a private house after the Dissolution of the monasteries

Opposite Maud Russell (far left) entertaining artists and philosophers in the garden at Mottisfont, including Freddie Ayer, Clive Bell and Angelica Garnett

shaping the natural beauty of the fertile land and harnessing the river to drive mills and provide food.

Today the River Test still flows through the estate and Mottisfont is again a place of pilgrimage for visitors who explore the house with its many layers of history, delight in the outstanding rose gardens and enjoy walks through its ancient woods and meadows.

A brief history

First came the hospitable Augustinians who received pilgrims eager to be blessed at the priory, where the forefinger of St John the Baptist was held as a sacred relic and where Peter de Rivallis (d.1262), the nephew of the Bishop of Winchester, was buried deep within the walls.

The Augustinian canons were forced to cede the priory in the Tudor era when statesman Sir William Sandys, a favourite of King Henry VIII, was given Mottisfont. Sandys made the existing church nave the base of his imposing new mansion, building additional wings either side.

In the Georgian period the house was transformed by the Barker Mill family, producing the façade you see today, and the estate was given over to hunting, shooting and fishing.

The last decades of the 19th century saw Mottisfont let to wealthy banker Daniel Meinertzhagen under eccentric terms that forbade the installation of electric light or central heating. The ten Meinertzhagen children included Daniel and Richard, who built aviaries for their extraordinary collection of eagles, hawks, owls and ravens.

The arrival of Mr and Mrs Gilbert Russell in 1934 made Mottisfont the centre of a fashionable artistic and political circle. Maud Russell, a wealthy patroness of the arts, created a substantial country house and sumptuously furnished it with early Regency antiques. In these lavish surroundings she entertained artists and writers such as Rex Whistler and Ian Fleming and many prominent figures, including the Churchills.

The source of the name
The Saxons held 'moots' or meetings and it is thought the name 'Mottisfont' means a meeting place by the 'font' or natural spring. The first mention of this 'font' is in Walter de Blount's Rental Book (see page 7), where we see that the priory used the water to manage watermills, orchards, gardens, a tannery and meadows.

The coming of the canons

The house at Mottisfont was never an abbey – that title came later – but rather an Augustinian priory, founded in 1201 by William Briwere, businessman, administrator and right-hand man to four Plantagenet kings.

Briwere became a rich man in royal service. He was one of the judiciaries left in charge of the kingdom when Richard I went on the Third Crusade in 1189 and later became a baron and trusted adviser to King John. In return he was given much land on which he levied substantial taxes, some of which was used to found four religious institutions – Torre Abbey and Dunkeswell Abbey in Devon, the hospital of St John in Bridgwater, Somerset, and the Priory of the Holy Trinity at Mottisfont.

Augustinian beginnings

A handful of canons lived at the Priory of the Holy Trinity. They were not cloistered monks but black-hooded Augustinian priests whose duty was to preach in the community, minister to those in need and welcome passing pilgrims. Mottisfont became an important stopping-off point for worshippers on their way to Winchester, especially as it was said to contain a relic believed to be the finger of John the Baptist, which had pointed out Christ as 'the light of the world'.

Generous hospitality

Throughout the century the Briwere family remained patrons of Mottisfont until the death of Patrick de Chaworth, a descendant, in 1297. His arms are carved into the archway leading from the kitchen. De Chaworth's daughter Maud, who is buried at Mottisfont, was a ward of Queen Eleanor of Castile, who generously endowed the priory and set up funds to feed poor widows on the estate.

This was a time of comparative prosperity. The great vaulted cellarium where the canons stored their food and drink can be seen today and it is not difficult to imagine the hospitality offered to visitors. Pilgrims on their way from Canterbury to Winchester would arrive dusty from the road, hungry and thirsty. After washing, they would sit with the canons to eat fish from the priory ponds or home-killed meat from the fields or dovecotes and drink beer, probably home-brewed. It was a sociable occasion as pilgrims, some of them bound for the shrine of St James in Santiago de Compostella in Spain, sat swapping travellers' tales. Guests would also listen to readings from the scriptures while they ate. After the meal, they would be offered a bed in a dormitory. Morning services were said in the priory church, the nave of which is incorporated in the house.

Above William Briwere's arms in the *pulpitum*, which was added to the priory in the 16th century, dividing the choir from the nave, now in the kitchen

Left Mottisfont gave food, shelter and blessings to passing pilgrims

Opposite The cellarium dates from the early 13th century and is the most complete part of the mediaeval monastic building to survive

The priory and prosperity

Eight centuries of history are buried deep within the walls of today's grand country house at Mottisfont and in the estate that surrounds it.

The vaulted cellarium, the giant 'larder' of the 13th-century priory, still stands. Traces of the mediaeval church, consecrated in 1224, and the priory cloisters, which were incorporated into the Tudor building, lie beneath the house.

Outside, the estate now comprises 1,645 acres (665 hectares) of meadow, woodland, park and gardens, the core of which was given by William Briwere when he founded the priory in 1201. A spring – the 'font' of Mottisfont – still bubbles through the ground. Wild brown trout swim in the Abbey Stream, which is a man-made diversion of the River Test, cut to feed watermills and possibly to supply water to the house.

Organisation

The 14th-century management of Mottisfont's lands is revealed by an account book compiled from 1340–5. It was ordered by one of the canons, Walter de Blount, the cellarer, who was not only in charge of the stores of food and drink but also responsible for recording the priory's considerable assets.

His Rental Book lists the spring (*fons* in Latin) that fed two watermills, two gardens, two courtyards, an apple yard and pasture, a meadow, a tannery and two dove houses. There were also a rabbit warren to the north of the house and a number of walnut trees. Records include a list of tenants, with particulars of their work on the estate.

And, just as importantly, the Rental Book offers clues about how the landscape of the estate was shaped. For example, it seems likely that bricks and tiles were made from local clay, while marl, a fertile soil used to dress the fields, was extracted, as were sand and gravel and also chalk, which was burned to make lime.

Natural resources

It is believed that the woodlands in the northern part of the estate were grazed by priory cattle. Once the land was exhausted, it was quarried and left to regenerate naturally. Today the Duck Grounds (north of the visitor car park) and garden are being restored with boardwalks and the removal of scrub and overgrown trees. This wet area of reed marsh, ponds and woodland, rich in flora and fauna, is the result of centuries of peat and marl extraction.

However the peaceful prosperity of the mid-14th century was not to last, but would be shattered by the Black Death.

Opposite Photograph showing parch marks that appear in dry weather that reveal the footprint of the vanished priory

Left A section of flint and stone wall dating back to the building's mediaeval and monastic origins

Right Walter de Blount's Rental Book

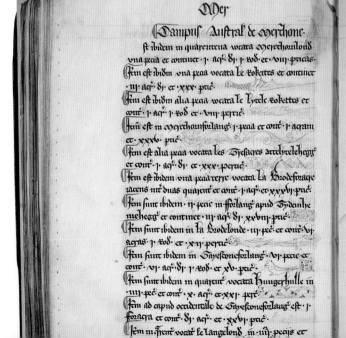

Disease, disaster and Dissolution

The Black Death, the terrible plague carried by rat fleas, hit England a little later than the rest of Europe. But when it reached this country in 1348 it spread with horrifying rapidity, killing more than a third of the population and wiping out entire towns and villages.

The death rate was often higher in religious institutions where clergy tended the sick and gave last rites to the dying. Walter de Blount, the Mottisfont cellarer, was one of the casualties. He had become prior in 1343, but fell victim to the deadly disease in 1349. His two successors, Robert de Bromore and Richard de Caneford, died in quick succession.

Uncertain footings

In 1352 Henry, Duke of Lancaster, the son of Maud de Chaworth (see page 5), asked the Pope to grant indulgences to all who visited the priory on feast days or who donated money. These paid-for 'penances' promised rewards in the after-life, such as a shorter stay in purgatory and salvation from hell.

But the good days were over. The death and destruction brought by the plague caused many to question the ways of the Church. Workers rebelled, no longer content to toil as serfs but wanting wages for their labour; lands were stolen and fell into disuse. By the early part of the 15th century the priory lands were being plundered and the fabric of the building itself was neglected and in need of repair.

Popes were becoming accustomed to pleas for financial help by beleaguered English priests, but in 1457 Pope Callistus III received an unusual request from the then prior, William Westkarre – an earthquake had struck Hampshire and had 'greatly crushed and loosened' the buildings.

Almost 30 years later, with the defeat of Richard III at the Battle of Bosworth in 1485, Henry VII, the first Tudor monarch, became king and it seemed for a while that happier times lay ahead for the struggling priory of which the new king was now patron.

Conversion

Henry planned to raise the priory's status to a Collegiate Church but this was never enacted. Shortly afterwards Mottisfont became a subsidiary of Westminster Abbey. In 1521 the priory gained a new patron, Henry Huttcroft. Considerable embellishments to the building followed, including the construction of the arched *pulpitum* (still in evidence between the old kitchen and the scullery) which divided the choir from the nave.

But the revival in the priory's fortunes was not to last. In 1536 the second Tudor monarch, Henry VIII, broke from the Roman Catholic Church and ordered his Chancellor Thomas Cromwell to dissolve all monasteries. In June of that year the estate became the property of William, Lord Sandys, who set about transforming the priory into a grand new house.

Opposite top Plague victims being blessed by a priest

Opposite bottom A section of the carved *pulpitum*, the screen that Henry Huttcroft had built to divide the choir from the nave

Right A 15th-century miniature called *The Fortress of Faith*, showing the Church under attack from secular quarters

William Sandys and the Tudor mansion

Below 18th-century engraving depicting the State Opening of Parliament in the reign of Henry VIII. One of those present is William Sandys, 1st Baron Sandys of the Vyne, Diplomat, Treasurer of Calais, Knight of the Garter

Lord Sandys, who had served as Henry VIII's Lord Chamberlain for five years, already owned The Vyne, a substantial manor house near Basingstoke in north Hampshire.

William Sandys, a personable diplomat in the court of King Henry VII, became a close friend of his second son, Prince Henry. When the young Henry was crowned king and married Catherine of Aragon, Sandys became a staunch supporter of the new queen. He was made Treasurer of Calais and, in 1518, a Knight of the Garter. Not long afterwards he used his diplomatic skills to smooth the way for the negotiations between Henry and Francis I of France at the Field of the Cloth of Gold.

Rewards for service

He was clearly influential at court and Henry and Catherine visited him at The Vyne in 1510. It was a measure of Sandys' friendship with the King that he managed to retain his favour even after the annulment of the royal marriage to Catherine. In 1535 Sandys, ever loyal, was required to receive Henry's new queen, Anne Boleyn, at his manor house.

Twelve months later the Mottisfont estate, the priory with its ruined outbuildings and the now redundant church were his. In exchange Sandys gave the villages of Chelsea and Paddington to the King. He was told he must build himself a great house, which is what he did, using the massive church building as the spine of his new home.

A suitably grand house

Lord Sandys was 66 years old when building started. Contemporary accounts say that he intended to live at Mottisfont for the rest of his life. But he died just four years later. An inventory, made on his death in 1540, suggests that structurally at least, the house was complete or nearly complete with a Great Chamber, an adjacent chamber and an Inner chamber over the nave of the church. A chapel was also mentioned, although its location is unclear.

Unusually for a Tudor house, there is no listing in that inventory of a Great Hall, a standard feature for the times. It is possible that Mottisfont was one of the first great houses in the country to have been built in a way that separated servants from the family.

Traces of Tudor

The only pictorial record of the Tudor house is shown on an estate map made in 1724. It was built around two courtyards, one formed from the old cloister. There appears to have been an L-shaped extension to the south, which might have been the main entrance.

Very little remains of the Tudor mansion, but fragments are visible in some of the door surrounds, glass, chimneys and fireplaces.

Above William Sandys was Knight of the Garter to Henry VII and subsequently to Henry VIII

Top right The estate map of 1724

Bottom right Close view of a glass and leaded light window

Below This herringbone design at the back of a fireplace is evidence of Lord Sandys' Tudor mansion

An 18th-century refurbishment

Mottisfont is one of a number of mansions created from the remains of monastic buildings after the Dissolution, but it is a notable example because of what has been saved of the original building.

Building began straight after Sandys' acquisition of Mottisfont, before the looting of valuable building materials could happen. Consequently he had the advantage of starting with a complete structure – the main part of the house was created out of the nave of the church – and much impressive mediaeval architecture remains.

Fluctuating fortunes

The Sandys family invested a great deal in their new house and estate, dividing their time between Mottisfont and their family seat, The Vyne. Records show that Queen Elizabeth I visited Mottisfont twice, in September 1569 and five years later in 1574, although we don't know if she slept here.

But, three-quarters of a century later, the country was riven by civil war and landowners were forced to choose between Cromwell and the King. Henry, the fifth Baron Sandys, fought for the King and died at the Battle of Cheriton in 1644. A decade later family fortunes had sunk so low that The Vyne was sold.

Towards the end of the 17th century the eighth and last Baron, Edwin, died childless and the title expired with him. Mottisfont's house and estate was left to his nephew, Sir John Mill in 1684.

Below The Tudor mansion was remodelled in the 1740s into a comfortable Georgian home

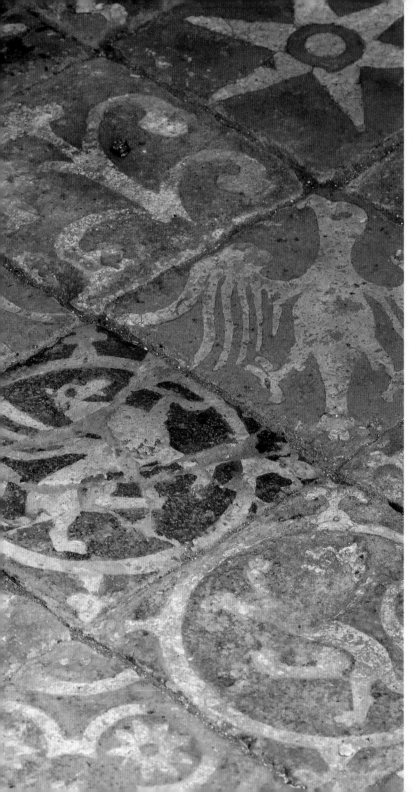

Favoured for eternity
William, third Baron Sandys, is buried in
the parish church of St Andrew, Mottisfont.
A brass plaque of 1628 on the floor beneath
the chancel arch incorporates a Latin
inscription that states his preference to
be buried *ad fontem* (at Mottisfont) rather
than *ad vitem* (at The Vyne).

The Mills of Mottisfont

The Mill family owned Mottisfont for two
hundred years and it was one of Sir John's sons,
Richard, who transformed the house into the
building we recognise today. Sir Richard,
Sheriff of Hampshire and a Member of
Parliament, built a three-storey Georgian
extension on the south side of the old Tudor
house. Although the interior has been much
altered by subsequent owners, the south front
we see today, with its pedimented roofline and
projecting end bays, has been subject only to
minor alteration.

Left Mediaeval floor tiles recycled to
pave the floor of the Summerhouse

Country pursuits

The 18th-century rebuild reflected change not only in fashion, but also in social structure. Kitchens were sited away from reception rooms, while back stairs and servants' quarters made the division between family and staff much more distinct.

Sir Richard demolished most of the Tudor buildings, but retained the arched windows on the ground floor and modified the Tudor stair turrets. As before, most of the existing mediaeval structure lay hidden behind the new rooms of the south front.

The sporting Sir John

Four sons and a grandson succeeded Sir Richard. Then, in 1835, the estate passed to a cousin, the Reverend John Barker, who promptly changed his name to Barker-Mill. A keen sportsman, known for his loud check trousers and cherry-coloured ties, he founded the Reverend Sir John Barker-Mill's Foxhounds (which later became the Hursley Hunt) and replaced the old stables at

Mottisfont with a fine new building in 1836, the year he received his baronetcy. He later gave up his hounds after complaints were made that the local fox population was declining too rapidly.

Quarters for horses

The Stable Block and pedimented Coach House with clock turret are arranged on three sides of a courtyard enclosed by a wall on the fourth. The gate into the yard is flanked by tall piers surmounted by carvings of chained and

Above *Mottisfont Abbey, View of the North and East Fronts*, a lithograph by G. F. Prosser from his *Select Illustrations of Hampshire* (1883)

Below The Stable Block, photographed in about 1880

Opposite The muzzled bear is from the coat of arms of the Mill family

muzzled bears from the Mill coat of arms.

Sir John was also a racing man and ran his stud here. It seems likely that he took over some of the ornamental parkland around the house as grazing for his horses. As a result of Sir John's extravagance at Mottisfont, some of the estate lands near Southampton had to be leased for revenue.

He left no children on his death in 1860 and his widow ran the estate for more than 20 years. In that time she founded the first school to be built in the village of Mottisfont.

Regency refrigerators

A cluster of recently planted holm oaks to the north-west of the Stable Block encloses a brick-built structure that served as a giant refrigerator in the late 18th and early 19th centuries. You can still see the Ice House, which was filled with tightly packed ice during the spring, making it cold enough to store winter game during the warmer spring and summer weather.

A family home

In 1884 Mottisfont became home to a large family – the ten Meinertzhagen children and their wealthy parents: Daniel, a banker and his wife Georgina, the sister of social reformer and co-founder of the London School of Economics, Beatrice Webb.

They took the house on a lease from its new owner, Mrs Marianne Vaudrey, a distant Barker-Mill cousin. Mrs Vaudrey (who later changed her name to Vaudrey-Barker-Mill) let Mottisfont at £320 a year with the condition that nothing in the house was altered and that neither electric lighting nor central heating should be installed.

Playtime at Mottisfont

The large family, with its wide and varied interests, loved both house and estate. The family photographs, copies of which are on display in the house, show many happy times: picnics, walks and rides, boating excursions on the river. Lively, intelligent and well-educated, the Meinertzhagen children – Daniel, Barbara, Richard, Margaret, Frederick, Lawrencina, Katherine, Louis, Mary and Georgina – grew up with a whole estate as their playground. Meanwhile, their parents enjoyed the company of political reformers, social thinkers and noted intellectuals including George Bernard Shaw, Charles Darwin, Cecil Rhodes, Henry ('Dr Livingstone, I presume') Stanley and philosopher Herbert Spencer.

Tall tales of derring-do

Colonel Richard Meinertzhagen, the second son and third child of the family, was celebrated during his life as a military hero and ornithologist. However, his stories of daring exploits may have been elaborations and do seem somewhat tall tales: he claimed to have killed seventeen Soviet agents in Spain and, on meeting Adolf Hitler, to have returned the 'Heil Hitler' salute with the words 'Heil Meinertzhagen'.

Lessons in nature

The eldest son, Dan, was just nine when his family moved to Hampshire. Here he and his younger brother Richard developed an avid interest in studying and collecting birds. Both boys were encouraged by Herbert Spencer, the sociologist and liberal theorist who is credited by Darwin as having developed the concept of the survival of the fittest. Spencer took Dan and Richard on long walks, urging them to 'Observe, record, explain!'

The pair took the study of birds seriously, building at least two aviaries which housed an extraordinary range of large birds, including Lobengula the sea eagle, Jacob the raven, two golden eagles, peregrine falcons, Belinda the kite and two white-tailed sea eagles.

Dan became an explorer and respected ornithologist, but died in 1898 at the age of just 23. It may have been this great loss and sorrow that led to the family leaving Mottisfont shortly afterwards.

Opposite **Pages from the Meinertzhagen family albums**

Top left **Dan with a wedge-tailed eagle**

Bottom left **Lobengula the sea eagle**

Vociferous Sea Eagle.
"Lobengula"

A 20th-century transformation

Like many Victorian matriarchs, Mrs Marianne Vaudrey-Barker-Mill had uncompromising views on many subjects, including the evils of drinking and gambling and, apparently, the debilitating effect of central heating.

After the departure of the Meinertzhagens, Mrs Vaudrey-Barker-Mill removed the central heating which they had installed contrary to the terms of the lease and spent £40,000 (the equivalent of £3 million today) restoring the house and estate. She owned land at Millbrook, Southampton, which she sold in order to raise finances.

Making more of the mediaeval

Mrs Vaudrey-Barker-Mill has been described as a 'hero of the Gothic' in her appreciation of the monastic history of the house. Her renovations exposed mediaeval masonry on the north and east fronts including a striking Early English (1200–1300) arch, formerly hidden by stucco on the north front and the archway that now frames the east entrance. By removing the parapet on the north side, she also exposed the roof of the old Sandys Great Chamber. She excavated a ramp that had hidden the undercroft of the priory chapter house and the remains of the dorter (dormitory) and demolished them to create an external staircase which leads up to the present-day Morning Room. The Long Gallery was redecorated and new staircases installed, but she still refused to contemplate electric lighting.

By 1908 the renovations were complete and Mrs Vaudrey-Barker-Mill let the house, furnished, for shooting parties but five years before she died, in 1932, the contents of the house were sold.

Modernising Mottisfont

The estate caught the eye of Gilbert Russell, a merchant banker, whose much younger wife

Above The illusionistic vaulted ceiling and pelmets of Maud Russell's saloon, painted by Rex Whistler

Left Mrs Vaudrey-Barker-Mill, who renovated Mottisfont and uncovered more of its mediaeval past

Maud was a society hostess and patron of the arts. Needing a country house where they could entertain weekend guests and where their young family could play, they bought Mottisfont in 1934 and started to breathe new life into the place.

At this time, the buildings were once again in a state of disrepair and the house lacked the modern conveniences required by a 20th-century family. Mr and Mrs Russell spent the next few years modernising the house and the estate. The exterior, apart from the addition of a new wing to accommodate servants of visiting guests, was little touched, but huge changes were made inside.

A woman's touch

Under Maud Russell's guidance, rooms were reconfigured and redecorated. Mrs Vaudrey-Barker-Mill's old, dark paintwork was replaced by light, pastel shades. Mrs Russell's approach appears to have been to build on the best of what she found. Inspired by the marbling in the Long Gallery, she added more; wooden chimneypieces were replaced with marble and new joinery was classical in style. Satin curtains swept down to the floor from swagged cornices above. Soft, fashionable felt carpets were fitted throughout. The house was furnished chiefly with high-quality early 19th-century antiques. The overall look was Neo-classical and luxurious.

Mrs Russell collected and supported the work of many artists. Just before war broke out in 1939, she transformed the original entrance hall into a large saloon, with French windows opening out onto a south-facing terrace. Rex Whistler was commissioned. The results were his spectacular *trompe l'oeil* murals, painted in a gothick style, light-heartedly reflecting the building's origins as a mediaeval priory. This extraordinary room was his last and finest piece before he was killed on active service in France.

A private joke
While Maud Russell was away for the weekend, Rex Whistler decided to embellish his paintings and at the same time tease her about her hatred of bonfires (the butler would be sent to put them out). Whistler's ermine-draped urn puffing out clouds of smoke sits in a *trompe l'oeil* alcove. It is surrounded by objects signifying Maud Russell's interests, including books and a lute (for music).

The Russells at Mottisfont

The spirit of Maud Russell, her vitality and artistic drive, can still be felt at Mottisfont. She arrived here in 1934. Lively, beautiful, with a strong aesthetic sense, she was greatly drawn to both the work and the company of creative people.

Artists, philosophers, designers and writers were the people whose company she enjoyed and whom she invited to stay. Rex Whistler, Russell Page, Geoffrey Jellicoe, Ian Fleming, Boris Anrep, Derek Hill and Norah Lindsay were all frequent visitors. She commissioned work from them and some became her very intimate acquaintances.

'Arrived at the Gilbert Russells'. Mottisfont is magnificent and romantic too. It is all stone, with rushing rivers, vast old yew trees, cedars, and lawns and a charming atmosphere of the past. Inside are long corridors, late Georgian white panelled rooms, beautiful mantelpieces and great comfort.'

Norah Lindsay, garden designer

Above **Mr and Mrs Gilbert Russell at Mottisfont**

Right **Guests relaxing in the Morning Room**

Opposite top **Maud Russell**

Opposite bottom **Monogrammed guttering bearing the Russells' initials**

A lover of art

Maud Russell was the daughter of Paul Nelke, a German Jew who established a successful stockbroking business in London before moving into personal banking. By the time she married Gilbert Russell, sixteen years her senior and cousin to the Duke of Bedford, in 1917, she was already respected for her knowledge of the contemporary art scene.

She owned a collection of modern French pictures including paintings by Pablo Picasso, Edgar Degas, André Derain and Amedeo Modigliani. She sat for William Orpen, Ben Nicolson, Henri Matisse and Boris Anrep, whose portrait of her in the role of 'Folly' can still be seen in the mosaics at the National Gallery.

Weekend retreats

Mr and Mrs Russell used the house mainly at weekends but a full staff (housekeeper, maids, kitchen maid, butler, chauffeur, gamekeeper and gardeners) kept the property running.

Typically, the Russells and their guests would arrive on a Friday evening. Preparations for an elaborate and beautifully presented dinner would have been under way all day. A dozen or more guests would sip their cocktails and nibble Maud's favourite cheese biscuit (made from ice-cream wafers, dipped in beaten egg, liberally coated with grated Parmesan and deep-fried) before being summoned to dinner.

Rest and relaxation

Mottisfont was never grand but it was always comfortable. Mrs Russell ensured her guests were able to relax, unwind and enjoy themselves. Long lie-ins, lazy breakfasts and the chance to join the shooting party, curl up and read, stroll around the grounds and enjoy sparkling conversation were all anyone had to do. Then there would be tea on the lawn or the terrace if the weather was good before dressing for dinner and gathering for cocktails in the saloon, now the Whistler Room.

Remembered in art
Fictional SIS agent James Bond, the creation of writer Ian Fleming, carried his gold-banded cigarettes in a heavy, monogrammed gun-metal case. At some time during the 1930s, Ian Fleming and Maud Russell became the sort of friends who gave each other special presents: he gave her an English version of Grivolin's *Breviary of Love*; she presented him with a heavy cigarette case of oxidised gold that resembled gun-metal. He used it always.

A haven for the arts

One of the most poignant sights at Mottisfont is a small 'incident' tucked high on the wall of Mrs Russell's grand saloon, now known as the Whistler Room.

Theatre designer, portrait painter, book illustrator and muralist Rex Whistler was commissioned to paint the room in a way that would deceive the eye.

There are no columns, ledges or moulded plasterwork in this room, the walls of which are so cunningly painted that they appear to have all these gothic decorations. On one of the *trompe l'oeil* 'ledges' stand a convincing paint pot and brush and box of matches, waiting for the return of the artist. Whistler left for France to fight in the Normandy Campaign of 1944, but never came back. Just 39, he was killed in action by a mortar on July 18.

Boris Anrep

Mrs Russell had many friends but her relationship with Russian mosaicist Boris Anrep turned into a long-lasting love affair. Anrep was part of London's artistic set and associated with the Bloomsbury Group from about 1912. He painted and wrote poetry, but is best known for his fabulous mosaics, which can be seen in London's National Gallery, the Bank of England and Westminster Cathedral. Maud Russell part-funded his work for the original entrance hall of the National Gallery and appears as the face of 'Folly' in the north vestibule. There are two examples of Anrep's work at Mottisfont:

one on the south elevation of the house, which depicts the figure of an angel bearing a very strong resemblance to Mrs Russell; the other is a small panel above the doorway in the Red Room, representing the Holy Trinity (see front cover).

Derek Hill

Another friend was the Hampshire-born painter and collector Derek Hill, who settled in County Donegal, Ireland. Hill spent much time at Mottisfont and became close to Mrs Russell. She commissioned works from him and it is through his generosity and the agency of The Art Fund that the National Trust is able to show at Mottisfont pictures by him and by other artists whose works he collected.

Above *Folly*, from Boris Anrep's mosaic on the north vestibule floor of the National Gallery, London, completed 1952

Opposite top Rex Whistler taking a break from the Mottisfont murals on the terrace

Opposite bottom left The Angel of Mottisfont by Boris Anrep

Opposite bottom right The paint brush and matches in Whistler's murals to which he never returned

Mrs Russell and Matisse

When Maud Russell sat for Henri Matisse in 1937, it must have been with a flutter of excitement that she entered his Paris studio in the Boulevard du Montparnasse. But sitting on a sofa for five consecutive mornings, trying to make conversation with the taciturn artist became wearisome and she was never happy with the large charcoal drawings, three of which were discarded. The remaining two were hung out of sight above the back stairs of her Hyde Park Gardens flat. They were sold at Sotheby's in 1985, three years after her death. She did revise her opinion of the artist (but never of the drawings) when he was her guest of honour at a London lunch party: he was charming and amusing, she reported.

The Derek Hill collection

Derek Hill, sometimes called the last of the gentlemen painters, was a talented landscape and portrait artist, capable of distilling the essence of his subject onto often small canvases.

He was rich enough to buy the works of painters who had influenced him, and sociable and thoughtful enough to encourage talent in others. His considerable art collection is split between his adopted country of Ireland and Mottisfont.

The artist

His family lived in the Dower House on the Mountbatten estate at Romsey, from where he was sent to Marlborough College to be educated. But he left school at 16, travelling to Russia, Germany, China and Italy to study theatre design. He worked for the Bolshoi Ballet, studied Bauhaus architecture in Hanover and began to paint in Paris,

Above The Quiet Wave by Derek Hill

encouraged by Edward Molyneaux whose collection of French Impressionist works excited him.

It is little wonder then that this empathetic and sociable raconteur loved invitations to Mottisfont, where Mrs Russell and her coterie enjoyed stories of his travels and the famous sitters he had painted.

When he needed solitude he found it on his beloved Tory Island off the coast of County Donegal in Ireland, the subject of many of his paintings. He supported and encouraged local artists, including the fishermen John and James Dixon, and eventually settled in Donegal.

The collection

Derek Hill died in July 2000, four years after a collection of 86 pictures, owned by him, was given to the National Trust through the Art Fund, to be displayed at Mottisfont. They cover not only his own work, including a

'A trip to Tory Island'
Derek Hill was once asked how he imagined death. 'Probably,' he said 'it will be like a trip to Tory Island'. Several of his Tory Island paintings can be seen at Mottisfont.

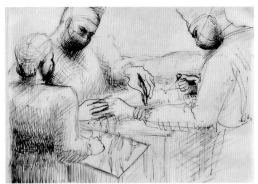

pencil drawing of Maud Russell and paintings of Tory Island, but also pieces by Modern Movement painters who had inspired him, such as Gwen and Augustus John, Ben Nicolson, Barbara Hepworth, Degas, L. S. Lowry, Edwin Landseer, Georges Seurat and Graham Sutherland.

There are also works by 'kitchen sink' painter John Bratby and Michael Andrews, both of whom he encouraged when he was director of the British School in Rome during the 1950s. Bratby's sketch of his first wife, the painter Jean Cooke, perhaps does not flatter her but shows a powerful personality.

It contrasts with Gwen John's quiet grey and blue pencil and gouache depiction of a house seen through a window, and Barbara Hepworth's pen and ink drawing of a surgical team at work, the fine lines of the images as precise as the operation itself.

Joan Eardley's *Cornfields, September* is a gem of a painting, revealing a tiny house, hidden in the glowing colours of the corn.

Above *Surgical Operation* by Barbara Hepworth (Bowness, Hepworth Estate)

Left *Cornfields, September* by Joan Eardley (with permission of the Eardley Estate)

The war years

The last years of Maud and Gilbert Russell's restoration of their country house were over-shadowed by the coming war. Mottisfont, as they wanted it to be, was completed just as the Second World War was declared and the house requisitioned.

The Russells lived for some time at a hotel in Brighton, but when Gilbert died in 1942 Maud moved to London to work for the Admiralty, travelling down to Mottisfont at weekends.

The Long Gallery became a hospital ward for non-critical war casualties. Up to 80 patients were looked after at any one time. Children, evacuated from London, lived in the Stable Block. Newspaper clippings showing the progress of the war can be seen fixed to the coach house wall.

It was not until after the war that Mrs Russell made Mottisfont her main home.

Continuity of care

The loss of her husband and the ravages of war must have made Mrs Russell aware of her own mortality. Anxious that Mottisfont should be preserved, she contacted the National Trust. Discussions followed over the next decade or so until 1957, when she gave the house and estate of 2,080 acres (842 hectares) to the Trust.

Mrs Russell continued to live at Mottisfont for another fifteen years, taking an active interest in estate and village life, continuing to walk in the middle of the road on her daily perambulations, refusing to deviate, so that motorists had to manoeuvre around her.

New owners

It was only when she moved to North End House in 1972, just across the road from the Walled Garden, that Graham Stuart Thomas, the Trust's first Gardens Adviser, decided that the central section of the Walled Garden was a suitable home for his collection of old-fashioned roses, then highly unfashionable plants. A tenant was found for the house which, other than the Whistler Room on Wednesday afternoons, was not open to the public.

Although Maud Russell had relinquished her use of the central part of the Walled Garden, she retained the northern section as an orchard, croquet lawn and general retreat, until a year or so before her death in 1982.

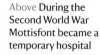

Above **During the Second World War Mottisfont became a temporary hospital**

Left **Maud (centre, clutching books) gathered with family members for Christmas at Mottisfont in 1946**

Right **Maud Russell presenting a token of gratitude to the tea lady of the cricket ground for 40 years of service**

Mrs Russell's resistance

Maud Russell never forgot her German-Jewish ancestry and, in the years leading up to the Second World War, helped several Jewish families escape from Nazi Germany, organising their accommodation once they reached England. She also flew to Frankfurt to arrange her relatives' departure and made plans for training Jewish youths for clandestine warfare at Mottisfont.

Care and conservation

Visitors to Mottisfont are impressed by the comfortable feel of the house, decorated by Maud Russell in an uncluttered and clean Neo-classical fashion.

The National Trust staff and volunteers in the house know exactly what many mean when they say that Mottisfont is a house they can imagine living in. 'I love to hear people imagining that they could live here. It isn't an overly grand house, but it has a quiet beauty,' says Kerry Bignell, House Steward. Kerry and her small team know Mottisfont Abbey better than most. They look after every inch of the rooms on display to the public, using special cleaning techniques developed by the National Trust to conserve materials, paintwork and fabrics.

The deep clean

During the short winter break they climb scaffold towers to reach the cornices. The deep clean starts at ceiling height and works down to the floor coverings. Special 'back pack' vacuum cleaners, with nozzles covered in muslin, are used in conjunction with pony hair or hog's hair brushes, so that dust is gently swept towards the cleaner and sucked away. Precious upholstery and fabrics are covered in a film of gauze before being lightly cleaned, the nozzle never touching the fabric.

Specialist care

Mottisfont is noted for the quality of its 'faux marbling' – a decorative paint technique that mimics the real thing. The walls of the Long Gallery, the Dining Room and the main staircase are covered in this special finish. Like all historic surfaces, it requires a lot of attention from experts, as the salts in the underlying stone leach out with the potential to break through and damage the delicate paints and glazes.

Many of the 'timberwork' finishes are actually paint applied to present a realistic grain and these too need special care, as does the ancient stonework.

The team looks after the famous Whistler Room (see page 19). The delicate murals are at constant risk of fading and abrasion and even small movements in the building can give rise to serious cracking. They have to be constantly monitored. The curtains in this room are now fragile, needing special treatment from a fabrics expert.

Now that the house is open for longer periods throughout the year, some of the conservation work is done in front of visitors so they can see the care taken in looking after these historic materials.

Right The wall decoration in the Dining Room is a faux marble finish that requires specialist conservation techniques

Hidden places

For some reason Maud Russell liked secret panels. There is one in the Green Library, where a push at the right place on one of the bookshelves once opened a hidden doorway into a guest bathroom. This opening in the panelling in the Yellow Room shows a part of the old priory building. Mrs Russell installed similar secret panels into her London home and into North End House, Mottisfont, when she moved there in 1972.

The Glory of the Garden

The abundant spring that encouraged settlement at Mottisfont hundreds of years ago is now an ornamental feature of the world-famous garden. The font and the River Test have enabled gardeners over the centuries to make a landscape that is both beautiful and productive.

We know that the canons of the 13th-century priory had two gardens and meadows where they would have reared animals and grown fruit, vegetables and herbs.

An early 17th-century survey and a 1724 estate map give clues about the layout of the pleasure grounds and park in the past, with formal avenues around the house, orchards to the north and south-west and fishponds. Gardens are mentioned in an early 18th-century survey around that time and it is thought there were parterres on either side of the house.

The 18th century

All this changed when Sir Richard Mill (see page 13) undertook his major refurbishment of the house and grounds in the mid-18th century. The formal avenues were replaced by a fashionable landscape park and it was at this time that many of Mottisfont's great trees were planted, including the sweet chestnuts which still stand along the drive. To the north of the house lay the pleasure grounds, while the rest became parkland or was laid to lawn and shrubberies. By 1791, the overall layout of the present landscape was in place. The walled kitchen garden (see over) appears to have been built towards the end of the 18th century.

The 20th century

Maud Russell commissioned some of the most influential English garden designers of the early 20th century, including Geoffrey Jellicoe and Norah Lindsay. Much of their work survives (see page 36).

Mrs Russell's strong sense of place clearly influenced the early 20th-century work. Just as the Whistler murals and the Anrep mosaics reflected the mediaeval and religious history of the site, so do the gardens. Norah Lindsay's box parterre, on the site of the old priory cloister on the south side of the house, is reminiscent of a mediaeval knot garden.

For work and play
The Abbey Stream was probably first cut in mediaeval times to bring water to the priory and its mills. It may have been reworked in the 17th century as a drainage channel for marshy ground between the house and the River Test. It is not known whether it was also purposely designed to be a feature of the pleasure ground, but it has certainly been used for recreation over the years and is still an idyllic place to walk and relax.

Jellicoe's north lawn (once a croquet lawn) with its cloister-like Lime Walk and terraces is only a short stroll from the Gothick Summerhouse on the east lawn. The 13th-century encaustic tiles on its floor were most likely introduced by Mrs Russell for that added mediaeval touch.

A pleasure garden

The Abbey Stream runs alongside the east lawn, made by man for reasons that appear both practical and decorative. Visitors are encouraged to walk along either side of the Abbey Stream as far as the rustic fishing hut (see page 50) with its quirky decorations of bark, which probably dates from the 19th century.

The original 18th-century parkland has been considerably reduced. What was the park now comprises the Stable Block, the main drive to the west gate, the Walled Garden and, further to the north, the 'Connygaer' or ancient rabbit warren and a clump of trees known as the 'Rookery'.

Opposite A statue of Apollo on the lawn to the north of the house

The Walled Garden

Mottisfont's Walled Garden has become world-famous for its sublime planting of old-fashioned shrub roses interplanted with herbaceous perennials.

The planting schemes were introduced from the 1970s, by the horticulturalist and rosarian, Graham Stuart Thomas, then the National Trust's Gardens Adviser. Until 1914, however, it was used for the purpose for which it was built – the production of fruit, vegetables and flowers for the house.

QUEEN PINE.

Exotic fruits

'The Pine-Apple is always in season at Mottisfont,' wrote an impressed William Thomson in 1869. Thomson was a significant figure in horticultural circles, a gardener himself, and writer and authority on the cultivation of grapes. In *The Gardener, A Magazine of Horticulture and Floriculture*, he describes four different types of 'Pine-Apple' grown in two large 'pine-pits' or hot beds. Black Jamaica, the Queen, Providence and the Cayennes were grown in succession.

There were also figs (Lee's Perpetual) fruiting three times a year from May, peaches, melons (Golden Queen and Bonsie's Incomparable, Broadland's Scarlet-fleshed and Malvern Hall) and strawberries which fruited from early March.

But best of all in Thomson's eyes was that Mottisfont had not the usual three glasshouses devoted to grape-growing, but four, demonstrating the head gardener's keen interest in viticulture. Thomson mentions varieties such as Black Hamburg, Muscadine and Buckland Sweetwater, Golden Champion, Mrs Pince's Black Muscat and Lady Downes.

The vineries, the other glasshouses containing peaches and figs, and the 'pine pits' were all in the frame yard, the southern section of the Walled Garden.

Left **The Queen pineapple**

> 'It is impossible to praise too highly the fine appearance of all the various departments, in or out of doors, at Mottisfont Gardens.'
>
> William Thomson, 1869

A fruitful plot

The kitchen garden, established in the late 18th century, was probably at its most productive during the time of the Reverend John Barker-Mill (see page 14). He died in 1860 but his widow took control until she died in 1884. An inventory of that time shows glasshouses used to produce bedding plants for the garden and flowering plants in pots, presumably for the house. Pictured is a detail from an Ordnance Survey map from 1871. The glasshouses had disappeared by 1967, but the Russells continued to use the Walled Garden to grow fruit and vegetables until the early 1970s.

Above right **The muscadine grape**

Left **The Walled Garden at Mottisfont** with white foxgloves in the foreground and dianthus-edged borders beyond

'Fine and abundant'

The area known today as the Rose Garden, with its central pond and quartered layout, was the old kitchen garden, the walls covered in fruit-laden trees with more planted in the open ground and in the northern section. Thomson notes a 'fine row of Pears, twenty-one in number, all of which are trained in a weeping form…'. He describes beds filled with 'vegetables of all descriptions, wondrous fine and abundant' and he was particularly impressed with the peas and beans: 'under some hand-lights were a lot of dwarf French Beans, to induce early fruiting; and on a warm border, fine well-filled pods of Sangster's No. 1 and Taber's Perfection Peas were ready for gathering'.

A garden of fine trees

Opposite The Lime Walk in autumn

Right A detail from the mosaic angel tablet, showing a tree, commissioned by Maud Russell from Boris Anrep

Below left The mighty plane tree that is in fact two grown together

Visitors approaching Mottisfont Abbey from the main car park often pause on the bridge over the Abbey Stream, from where they catch their first glimpse of the house. At the same time they see an enormous tree which, from some angles, seems to dwarf the building.

This is in fact a pair of trees, once quite clearly separate but now growing closely together to stand at least 34 metres (111 feet) tall. The huge trees are part of a collection of planes, probably planted in the first half of the 19th century by the Reverend Sir John Barker-Mill (see page 14).

It is likely that many of Mottisfont's other significant trees, including the horse chestnut (*Aesculus hippocastanum*) near the Walled Garden, are from this period, although the fine sweet chestnuts (*Castanea sativa*) lining the upper part of the drive are mid-18th century plantings. The cedars of this period have been lost, many having been blown down during a great storm in 1928. The replacements are thought to have been planted by Maud and Gilbert Russell just before the Second World War.

The venerable oak tree seen on the east lawn pre-dates the chestnuts by several hundred years, while other trees of note include both purple and green beech, holm oak, hornbeam, tulip trees (*Liriodendron tulipifera*), walnut, Indian bean or cigar tree (*Catalpa speciosa*) and examples of bird cherries (*Prunus padus*), black mulberry and crab apple.

Successional planting

While these specimen trees are fine examples of the type of carefully planned 'informal' landscape planting of the end of the 18th and 19th centuries, the elegant double row of pollarded limes and the yew octagon (see page 37) to the north of the house were planted later, in Maud Russell's time. They contrast with the natural growth of the chestnuts and beech. A beech circle was also planted between the Walled Garden and the Stable Block about 50 years ago to replace a similar feature near the Ice House that had come to the end of its life.

Forever at Mottisfont
Mottisfont's last private owner, Maud Russell and her lover, the Russian mosaicist Boris Anrep, are rumoured to have planted two trees in the grounds under which they wanted to be buried. In the event, Mrs Russell was interred in her family mausoleum, although it is thought that Anrep's ashes were scattered in the grounds.

A 20th-century design

While Mottisfont's great trees bear testimony to 18th- and 19th-century planting, much of what today's visitors admire in the garden was established under the direction of Maud Russell.

Mrs Russell commissioned leading designers Norah Lindsay and Geoffrey Jellicoe to introduce formal elements of design to the garden and Russell Page to suggest plantings.

Norah Lindsay

Norah Lindsay was an aristocrat, married to the son of the Earl of Crawford. They lived at Sutton Courtenay, where she created a garden of some renown. She was much influenced by the gardens of Persia with their free-growing fragrant roses and by contemporary garden designer, Gertrude Jekyll.

She moved in high social circles, in which her advice on gardens was much sought. When her marriage failed and she fell on hard times, she decided to design and create gardens professionally, enlisting her friends as clients. Among others she worked for the Astors at Cliveden and Philip Kerr at Blicking Hall, both now National Trust properties.

The pattern of her box-edged parterre on the south lawn at Mottisfont reflected the design of a window (now altered) over the nearby central door. Lindsay decreed that the compartments were to be filled with blue and cream bedding plants in spring and yellow and mauve in summer.

Above Norah Lindsay's box-edged parterre was designed to reflect and complement the architecture of the house

Left Socialite turned garden designer, Norah Lindsay

It is very likely that Lindsay had a strong influence on the design and planting of the double-sided ornamental borders in the central Walled Garden, now the main Rose Garden. However, as she seldom produced planting plans, it is difficult to be sure of her exact involvement. Borders on a north-south axis either side of the path are typical of Lindsay's distinctive design and planting style.

Like Vita Sackville West at Sissinghurst Castle and, later, Graham Stuart Thomas (see page 38), Lindsay worked in a painterly style. She used plants for their texture, shape and colour, and grouped them in natural-looking drifts. She loved old varieties of roses and understood that they grew in harmony, their short flowering season framed by herbaceous perennials.

Geoffrey Jellicoe

Geoffrey Jellicoe was emerging as one of the foremost designers of the day when he became involved at Mottisfont. He had originally trained as an architect but, influenced both by Italian Renaissance gardens (on which he wrote a book with Jock Shepherd) and later by the Modern Movement, he forged a high-profile career as a landscape architect, and is now widely regarded as the leading British landscape architect of the 20th century.

In spite of his credentials, Mrs Russell was absolutely clear about what she wanted and

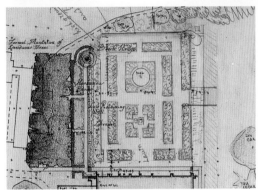

Above Acca (*Feijoa sellowiana*), one of the planting recommendations made by Russell Page in the 1930s, still thriving at Mottisfont today

Left G.A. Jellicoe & Partners' 1936 design for the formal gardens to the north of the house, annotated 'Jellicoe's Plan for the Garden. Not carried out. M.R.'

Below left Geoffrey Jellicoe, the leading British landscape architect of the 20th century

rejected Jellicoe's first designs for an elaborate parterre garden on the north lawn. She did accept his proposal for a pleached (where branches are interwoven) Lime Walk, however she insisted that the whole design was reversed, so that the yew octagon was located at the southern, not the northern, end of the limes.

Russell Page

Russell Page, originally a painter, was also influenced by Italian Renaissance gardens. In 1938 he was approached to recommend shrubs for the garden. Many of his recommendations, including the rare *Schizofragma integrifolium*, acca (*Feijoa sellowiana*) and *Hoheria lyalii* are still flourishing today.

Graham Stuart Thomas

Graham Stuart Thomas OBE wanted only a life working with plants. Born in 1908, he worked as a volunteer at the Cambridge University Botanic Garden, eventually becoming a partner at Sunningdale Nurseries and a garden designer just after the Second World War.

GST, as he came to be known, was a good artist and photographer, often illustrating his planting plans for private clients with his pen and camera, later using the same skills when his acclaimed books on roses were published.

His love of all plants was consuming, but when it came to roses – especially the old shrubs and climbers which had gone out of fashion – his enthusiasm knew no bounds. He began to make a collection of old roses, at that time deeply out of fashion. It would not be an understatement to say that he saved them.

A flourishing career

In 1948 Lawrence Johnston gave his Arts and Crafts garden, Hidcote, to the National Trust. This was their first great garden and they called upon GST for advice. In 1955 he was officially appointed Gardens Adviser to the Trust, working in later years as a consultant, until his death in 2003. GST received many awards, including the Veitch Memorial Medal from the RHS in 1966, the Victoria Medal of Honour in 1968 and an OBE for his work with the National Trust.

By the early 1970s he was looking for a new home for his outstanding collection of old-fashioned shrub roses and, naturally, he turned to the Trust. Several properties were considered but Mottisfont was chosen, and in 1972–3 he moved the roses into the walled central section of the former kitchen garden.

Setting the scene

In his book *An English Rose Garden* (1991) GST writes: 'We are now at the garden door. Few better sites could have been found for a garden of old roses than this. It is roughly square with cross-paths meeting at the central pool and fountain guarded by eight Irish Yews.

Following the line of the old soft-toned, red-brick walls are gravel walks hedged with box. In the middle of each quarter of the whole plot is a small rectangular lawn. There were several old apple trees which make good hosts for climbers. The main path from the garden door leads to an arch in the distant wall and the whole walk is given almost entirely to four borders of hardy plants of soft colours. Only at the very beginning of borders are a few strong colours allowed to give point to the general scheme.'

Dedication

In the opening section of *An English Rose Garden* Graham Stuart Thomas reveals that the soil in the kitchen garden was hungry and extremely stony. There was no access through the narrow doorways for machinery or loads of manure, so everything had to be done 'by barrows and hand-digging'. Perhaps that is one of the reasons the book is dedicated to David Stone, Mottisfont's Head Gardener for well over 30 years.

Above This many-petalled golden-yellow rose is a special feature at the entrance to the Rose Garden. It is named 'Graham Stuart Thomas' in honour of the great plantsman and rosarian

Opposite *Rosa gallica versicolour* (*Rosa mundi*) gallica ancient

Left Graham Stuart Thomas

The Rose Garden

The gardens at Mottisfont Abbey are a year-round attraction. However, during June, when their unrivalled collection of old-fashioned roses fills two walled gardens with scent and dazzle the eyes with colour, it is an unforgettable experience.

These roses have a historical importance beyond their beauty. They were collected by the late Graham Stuart Thomas, plantsman, writer, artist, photographer and rosarian par excellence. GST was Gardens Adviser to the National Trust from 1955 to 1974 and a major influence on many of Britain's great gardens. Mottisfont is the most complete example of his work that survives intact.

A dazzling display

He not only established a comprehensive collection of pre-1900 shrub roses during the 1970s, but also displayed them in what was then an innovative fashion. With an artist's eye and consummate knowledge, GST planned a garden that would combine roses with a mix of perennials to give a season-long display.

A gateway set in a sunny rose-covered wall leads to the first Rose Garden with deep box-lined borders full of rambling and climbing roses and clematis on the high brick wall behind. The main paths crossing the site converge on a central round pond and fountain surrounded by eight clipped Irish yews.

Long borders brim with plants chosen to complement and underplant the roses. They also extend the season, providing colour, shape and scent before the roses bloom and after their petals fall. In June the roses are accompanied by striking spires of white foxgloves.

The northern section of the Walled Garden, with its wide paths, is deliberately planted with a 'cool' colour palette to provide a counterpoint to the central Rose Garden.

Left White bench with rambler rose Adelaide d'Orleans over the wooden pergola in the Rose Garden

Right Bleu Magenta and Debutante climbing over pergolas create a glorious summer spectacle

Learning and discovery

When he arrived at Mottisfont in 1978, David Stone knew as much as any head gardener about old roses, with their intensely coloured flowers and wonderful scent. That knowledge, he freely admits, did not amount to much, as they were rarely grown at that time. He worked closely with Graham Stuart Thomas and became an authority on the hundreds of varieties in Mottisfont's collection. 'GST's great strength was his scholarly knowledge and ability to identify roses correctly,' said David. 'He discovered many, including the true musk rose [*Rosa moschata*, pictured], and "Indigo", a Portland rose thought to be lost.'

The Winter Garden

As Mottisfont welcomes visitors throughout the year, a garden designed to delight all the senses in autumn and winter has been planned and planted. The one-acre Winter Garden took shape in 2010 near the site's oldest feature, the font, which attracted settlement here more than 800 years ago.

Gravel paths wind through winter-flowering shrubs and perennials, chosen for colour and scent. There is an emphasis on plants such as dogwood and ornamental bramble with brilliantly coloured winter bark. A wet area near the font supports ornamental willow, the stems of which take on burgundy, russet or yellow tints in the winter months.

Scent, colour and structure

Sweet-scented daphnes and winter-flowering honeysuckles, wintersweet, witch hazel and bright mahonia, whose flowers have a lily-of-the-valley smell, and viburnum all contribute to a subtle fragrance in the crisp cold air.

Bright berries and fruit are provided by skimmia and euonymus, while late- and early-flowering perennials such as bergenia and hellebores also provide colour during the shortest days of the year.

A ribbon of clipped buxus threads its way down a steep slope, while 'streams' of ground-hugging periwinkle, pachysandra and early spring bulbs echo the flow of the water from the adjacent font.

The pleasure grounds

The Winter Garden is just one example of the Trust's commitment to presenting our natural and cultural heritage in imaginative ways. Likewise, but many more years in the making, Maud Russell's pleasure grounds aspired to a combination of natural beauty and reflected history.

The pleasure grounds are dotted with historic statues and garden features. Maud Russell bought the four stone figures, or herms, that once adorned a Roman bath-house, and introduced the two 18th-century Coade stone urns that stand at the entrance to the east porch.

The Gothick Summerhouse that sits on the north lawn may have been a feature since the 18th century but has almost certainly been rebuilt, probably in the 19th century. Inside are a number of 13th-century coloured clay tiles, dating from the early days of the priory, but which were probably laid down in the early 20th century. Similar tiles exist in Winchester Cathedral and the church of the St Cross Hospital.

Opposite top *Daphne bholua* 'Jaqueline Postill'

Opposite bottom Angus Menzies, a Russell family friend, gazing at his reflection in the font

Above right The detail of vines on this stone urn is suitable decoration in the pleasure grounds

Left One of four herms, bought by Maud Russell, that once stood in a Roman bath-house

Resting places
The small memorial stones to one side of the Summerhouse mark the final resting place of pets belonging to Mrs Vaudrey-Barker-Mill and the Meinertzhagen family. Behind the Summerhouse is a stone coffin found beneath the floor of the church nave when the National Trust refurbished the house in the late 20th century.

The Estate

When the Priory of the Holy Trinity was established at Mottisfont at the very beginning of the 13th century, a productive estate developed on the land with which it was endowed.

Today's 1,645-acre (665-hectare) estate, owned and managed by the National Trust, is still shaped by the way the priory lands were used, although considerable changes occurred in the 19th century when the estate's opportunities for sport dominated its use.

From those early days until comparatively recently, clay (for brick making), chalk, sand, gravel, marl and peat have been dug out of the land, leaving sunken areas such as the Duck Grounds. The woods were coppiced, presumably for timber and fuel as there is no evidence of charcoal burning in the area.

Fields were enclosed and water meadows and hedgerows established in the 17th century, suggesting that farming, both livestock and arable, became an important feature of estate activity. The fields and hedges we see today probably date from this period. It seems likely that a water mill was still in use right up to the 19th century.

Used for sport

When the sporting Reverend Sir John Barker-Mill inherited in 1835, a different emphasis was brought to the management of the estate. Farming and brick making continued but Sir John (see page 14) acquired more land and made hunting, shooting and fishing (especially hunting) a priority. He ran shoots through the woods and established fishing beats on the Test ensuring the Mottisfont estate gained a reputation for good sport.

Sir John's successors, the lively and numerous Meinertzhagens, who rented the house, land and fishing rights for £320 a year

from Mrs Marianne Vaudrey-Barker-Mill, carried on the sporting tradition. Photographs from this period show shooting parties, while in his *Diary of a Black Sheep* (1964) Richard Meinertzhagen (see page 16) recalls 'shooting, fishing, hunting and eternal messing about with water'. He remembers, 'The shooting at Mottisfont was naturally good, and … included some of the best partridge ground in Hampshire.'

The Russells, who arrived in 1934, kept a gamekeeper and established a weekend shoot for their guests, but Mottisfont's heyday as a sporting estate was over.

Above A shooting party at Mottisfont c.1915

Opposite View over fields behind the Stable Block

Childhood reminiscences
Richard Meinertzhagen's diaries reveal that when he revisited Mottisfont in 1942, seeking memories of his childhood, he made his way to the Duck Grounds, where he and his brother, Daniel, had built a water aviary. There, at the base of a maple tree, he discovered 'an old rusted saucepan, two tins of sardines and a pot of jam, just as Dan and I had left them in 1897'.

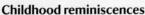

The village

With the exception of St Andrew's Church, little in the village is as old as the priory, but some buildings can be dated from the 14th century, telling the story of a community that grew up around a thriving estate.

St Andrew's Church, which is Grade I listed, possibly predates the priory by 50 years or so, although it underwent rebuilding in the 15th century. Today at least 60 cottages – most of the village – are part of the Mottisfont estate and are home to National Trust tenants.

These estate cottages tell the story of English vernacular architecture from the 14th to mid-20th century, using every material available: timber, chalk, cob, local Michelmersh brick, tile, slate and lime render. The tradition of thatching continues today with long wheatstraw thatch, although there is evidence that one cottage in Church Lane was once thatched with river reed.

Abbey Farm Cottages and Dairy Cottage near the west entrance of the abbey are unusual in that they are as Wealden houses: mediaeval timber-framed buildings, normally found in Kent and Sussex.

Building a community

The National School, founded in 1872 by Sir John Barker-Mill's widow and enlarged in 1889, closed in 1982. The shop and post office have also closed but the old school building still serves the community as a village hall. The old village pub, The Fox, was closed by Mrs Vaudrey-Barker-Mill at the beginning of the 20th century and is now a tenanted house.

Below The buildings of Mottisfont village preserve a long and varied history of English rural architecture

There was a spate of building in the 17th century, possibly coinciding with the Sandys family's decision to sell The Vyne and focus their energies and finances on Mottisfont. Gradually timber frames gave way to brick-based construction and clay roof tiles appeared on buildings such as Oakley Farmhouse, Trokes Cottage and The White House.

Few new buildings went up in the 18th century, although a smithy, since disappeared, operated in Hatt Lane at this time. Building increased in the 19th century, with some variety creeping into style. Simple brick cottages with clay-tiled roofs dominated, but Glebe Farmhouse, built in Regency Gothic, was evidently of a comparatively high status in the village, as was the Rectory (not National Trust). Cob and chalk walls with thatch continued to be used for humbler dwellings, such as the almshouses. In the Edwardian period semi-detached, workers' cottages were built by Mrs Vaudrey-Barker-Mill, after which there was a lull. In the 1930s further housing in brick and tile was added by the Russells, incorporating the then-fashionable metal-framed Crittall windows, associated with the Art Deco movement and which remain in some of the houses.

Village business

Like so many villages, Mottisfont has lost much of the business it used to support. The Andover and Redbridge canal once ran through Mottisfont. This was completed by the end of the 18th century. It connected Andover to Southampton, and would have been a busy trade route. Later the canal was converted to a railway line, completed in 1865, which became known as the 'Sprat and Winkle Line'. Mottisfont even had its own station. The station buildings are still standing today, but they are now private houses. Most of the line, including the part that served Mottisfont, was closed in the 1960s.

Above left Children outside a thatched cottage, now demolished, c.1918

Above right An estate cottage and workers, c.1920

The River Test, which flows through Mottisfont, has shaped the estate through the centuries and is the bright thread that binds the history of the house and its people to the landscape.

The Test, one of the great chalk streams of the world, has played a significant part in making Mottisfont what it is. With crystal clear waters fed by springs filtered through chalk from underground aquifers, it is the perfect habitat for wild trout and salmon.

A rich environment
The 'font' or spring which gives Mottisfont its name is a natural feature, fed by the river. The rich, moist soil in the valley area around the Test and its tributary, the Dun, produces the flower-filled meadows and lush common land that today's visitors enjoy. The reedy areas, fens and ditches around the rivers are exceptionally rich in wildlife, much of which is rare and endangered (see page 54).

The water meadows, introduced in the 17th century for both arable and livestock farming, are good examples of a traditional feature that is becoming increasingly rare in Britain. The meadows, drainage ditches and ancient ponds give clues to the past use of the land.

The Duck Grounds to the north of the visitor car park lie in a deep bowl created by peat extraction long ago. Now it is an area of ponds,

Above Anglers have been coming to Mottisfont for generations

Opposite Chalk streams are noted for their clarity

streams, reed beds and marsh, supporting an extraordinary range of flora and fauna. It lies between the Test and the Abbey Stream, and was once a shooting ground for duck and was where the Meinertzhagen brothers, Daniel and Richard, (see page 17) built a water aviary in 1893.

Working and playing with water
The Abbey Stream is a man-made water channel, probably first cut in mediaeval times to bring water to the priory and to power watermills. It is thought that it was reshaped in the 17th century to drain nearby marshy ground and possibly to make it more of a landscape feature in the pleasure grounds. Late 19th-century photographs show boating parties on the wide stream (see page 31).

The Test is world-renowned for brown trout fishing. The four 'beats' or fishing stretches (one of them on the River Dun) are managed by the National Trust and leased to the Mottisfont Fly Fishing Club. They not only provide world-class sport but also have historic associations with the father of dry fly fishing, Frederic Halford (see over).

The journey of the Test
The Test rises at Ashe, west of Basingstoke and flows for 64 kilometres (39 miles) through Hampshire to drain into Southampton Water. Tributaries include the Dever, Anton and Wallop Brook and the Dun. The four fishing beats on the estate are known as The Main, Rectory, Oakley Stream and The Dun. The Dun joins the Test below the central settlement in Mottisfont.

Fly fishing on the River Test

Anglers the world over know of the River Test. It is one of the most famous chalk streams, renowned for the quality of its dry fly fishing.

The River Walk from the house leads to a thatched fisherman's hut, where traditionally anglers could store their equipment, take a break from fishing, or shelter from the worst of the weather. It features the depiction of a bear, from the Mill family coat of arms. Circular thatched huts like this one are characteristic features of the Test, where today they continue to provide shelter, somewhere to eat, brew tea, or simply to sit and enjoy the riverside landscape.

Frederic Halford

The thatched Oakley Hut, on the bank of the Oakley Stream on the estate, is famous for its connection with W. Frederic Halford, one of the great names in the annals of fly fishing. It was here, at Mottisfont, that Frederic Halford promoted and perfected the art of dry fly fishing.

Halford came from a wealthy clothes-manufacturing family in the Midlands. He was taken fishing for the first time when he was just six and spent his childhood trying to outwit pike, barbel, perch and chub. In his early twenties he began to fish the Wandle in south-west London, using a hickory rod with a silk and horsehair line. He had little success with wet fly fishing but immediately took to the dry fly method. (Dry flies are designed to be fished dry so that they float on the surface of the water, whereas wet flies are fished wet and under the surface of the water.) In his

Above Fisherman's hut on the river's edge

Left Frederic Halford tying flies

Below *Floating Flies and How to Dress Them* (1886)

FLOATING FLIES
AND HOW TO DRESS THEM
A TREATISE
ON THE MOST MODERN METHODS OF DRESSING
ARTIFICIAL FLIES FOR
TROUT AND GRAYLING
WITH FULL ILLUSTRATED DIRECTIONS AND CONTAINING
NINETY HAND-COLOURED ENGRAVINGS OF THE
MOST KILLING PATTERNS
TOGETHER WITH A FEW
HINTS TO DRY-FLY FISHERMEN
BY
FREDERIC M. HALFORD

LONDON
SAMPSON LOW, MARSTON, SEARLE, AND RIVINGTON
CROWN BUILDINGS, 188, FLEET STREET
1886
(All rights reserved)

autobiography he wrote of his joy as he watched trout rising to 'upright-winged floating duns'. He remained devoted to dry fly fishing for the rest of his life.

Halford is sometimes credited with inventing dry flies. He didn't but he did more than anyone to promote and teach the method.

Perfecting his art

In 1877 he joined the Houghton Club on the Test and a couple of years later, in a Winchester fishing shop, met George Selwyn Marryat, reckoned by many to be the greatest fly fisherman of the time. Their friendship and collaboration lasted until Marryat's death at the age of 56. Together they researched and wrote *Floating Flies and How to Dress Them* (1886), although the publicity-shy Marryat declined to be named as co-author.

The book was an instant success and Halford wrote six more books and at least 200 articles for *The Field*, under the byline 'Detached Badger'.

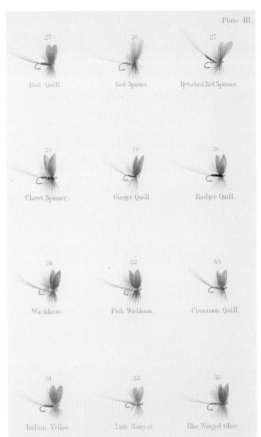

Floating Flies and How to Dress Them (1886)
This book provides an in-depth study of nearly 100 duns and spinners in the English chalk streams of Hampshire County.
The book contains detailed drawings and instructions on how to create hand-made artificial flies and is illustrated with plates showing flies such as the Red Spinner, Wickham, Indian Yellow, Little Marryat, Blue Winged Olive, Bumbles and Red Tags.

Left Twig work on the fisherman's hut

Modern management

Ensuring a habitat for wildlife is at the heart of management of the 1,645-acre (665-hectare) Mottisfont estate. Its ancient woodland and river valley are managed to create a species-rich habitat that visitors can enjoy all year round.

Two tenanted farms, Hatt Farm (mixed arable) and Newlyns (beef), keep the agricultural tradition going. The National Trust keeps Highland cattle and sheep as 'lawnmowers' and weed clearers.

There is no hunting or shooting for sport on the estate now, but there is still fishing on historic parts of the Test.

Managed for access

The countryside team at Mottisfont looks after the walks open to members of the public. There's a six-mile (ten-kilometre) estate walk and a cycle route which starts at Keepers Lane in the village. Small car parks serve Great Copse and Spearywell Woods, which are open to walkers. Both these areas of ancient woodland, like the rest of the woodland on the estate, are managed for wildlife, particularly butterflies and rare bats. 'Crop' trees such as conifers are gradually being removed to encourage naturally regenerating broadleaved trees, primarily oak.

Managed for wildlife

Centuries ago the River Test would have flowed in a wider, shallower channel, making a floodplain across the meadows to the north of the house. It is believed the Augustinian canons diverted and canalised it and, over the centuries, others have modified it further for domestic use. Now the Trust plans to reconnect the river to its landscape, allowing the waters to escape into the surrounding fields, re-creating the water meadows first introduced in the 17th century and restoring a marshy habitat. This in turn will attract much more wildlife, including threatened wading birds such as redshank, curlew, snipe and lapwing and the insects and invertebrates on which they feed.

The countryside team ensures that arable meadows are kept well away from the river, so that there is no danger of fertiliser or sediment leaching into the water.

The annual weed cut

Every two weeks in June, July and August river keepers undertake the annual weed cut on the river to manage water levels, as a flood defence and to maintain conditions as a habitat for fish and other water creatures. They don waders for the task or take to the water in boats. The tonnes of cut weed are collected further down the river at Greatbridge. This is a long tradition, as is shown in this photograph of 74-year-old William Lickman with his assistant Joe Smith cutting weeds on the River Test to ensure that the beats are in perfect condition for fly fishing.

Top **Snipe**

Above **Curlew**

Opposite **The River Test** is the perfect habitat for wild trout

A haven for wildlife

Mottisfont with its ancient woodland, river, meadows and wetland is home to an enormous range of wildlife, from the elusive otter to the tiny and extremely rare fine-lined pea mussel.

Few visitors will see the pea mussel or the equally endangered Desmoulin's whorl snail, both found in drainage ditches on the estate, but there is a chance some may glimpse one of Mottisfont's most welcome species, the scarce barbastelle bat. Only a few colonies of this small mammal exist in the British Isles and it is

On red alert
The International Union for the Conservation of Nature (IUCN) publishes a 'Red List' of endangered species of flora and fauna. Many of the creatures on the list can be found at Mottisfont, including lapwing and the barbastelle bat (pictured).

feared that they are on the decline.

The diet of these bats consists mainly of moths and the occasional spider, which they catch as they swoop low over the river and tree tops. Mottisfont's wooded river valley is an ideal hunting ground. In winter they tuck themselves into the shelter of hollow trees and roost under loose bark in the spring and the autumn. They mate in the autumn and in early summer the pregnant females congregate in small maternity roosts in the woods where they each produce a solitary offspring in June. Barbastelle bats differ from all other bats in that their ears are fused together on their foreheads.

There are nine other species of bats roosting on the estate, including pipistrelles, noctules and Daubentons.

Rare species
Less than 30 years ago, water voles were considered a common species, but now they are endangered and protected. They are known to inhabit parts of the River Test to the east of the house. Otters can occasionally be

Above **Mottisfont in May**

Above right top **Water vole** (*Arvicola terrestris*)

Above right bottom **Pea mussel** (*Pisidium amnicum*)

Opposite **Reed bunting** (*Emberiza schoeniclus*)

Below **Purple emperor** (*Apatura iris*)

seen on the same stretch of river, while dormice also breed here. Dragonflies thrive along the water meadows and river.

As well as the moths which are eaten in great numbers by the barbastelle bats, Mottisfont supports several rare species of butterfly, including the purple emperor. White admirals, Duke of Burgundy fritillaries and silver-washed fritillaries, also scarce, have been found in woodland areas on the estate.

Birds of Mottisfont

A wide range of birds flourish in the diverse ecosystem found at Mottisfont. Kingfishers hunt along the river and water rail, shy birds with a squealing call, also thrive here. Nightingales, whose song is more pleasant, can be heard, while lapwings, another protected species, are also known to breed here. Barn owls swoop over the night-time landscape and nest in trees and old buildings.

The English or grey partridge with its distinctive orange 'cheeks' and reed buntings, another declining species, can also be spotted at Mottisfont.

Mottisfont now

Mottisfont is an ancient place. We only know what happened here during the last 800 years, but its history extends much further back. We, like those whose stories we have been telling in this guidebook, are simply passing through.

The Augustinian priors, who established the community here and fashioned the working landscape, may have believed that their way of life would continue until the end of the world, but it ended violently, surviving the Black Death but falling to the Dissolution.

They were followed by the Tudor statesman Lord Sandys and a long line of his descendants. The Mill and Barker-Mill families turned the priory into a splendid house and the estate into a prosperous and productive network of farms and sporting grounds over a period of more than three centuries.

Although in residence for just fifteen years, the Meinertzhagens left photographs and diaries recording times spent having fun on the estate. But Mr and Mrs Gilbert Russell's lifestyle and love of art are still palpable in the very fabric of Mottisfont. Their respect and understanding of its past is reflected in their sensitive additions to both house and gardens.

It is because Mrs Russell believed that Mottisfont should be cherished forever that the latest chapter in the history of the estate began – its ownership by the National Trust.

A continuous flow

The font that gives name to the place still flows, and the estate is constantly evolving. The gardens have their seasonal flourishes, particularly the Rose Garden and the Winter Garden, and the house, in keeping with the support Mrs Russell gave to artists, has a changing programme of exhibitions.

Many layers of history can be glimpsed at Mottisfont. It has been shaped by countless hands and still has the ability to touch all sorts of visitors.

Above **Picnics before an open-air theatre performance**